my cat forgets who pays the rent

pictures and verse
by
Sandra Magsamen

gift

stewart tabori & chang

I'd like to
introduce
my cat to
you.

Perhaps you know one like this too.

My cat is
beautiful . . .
like a movie
star.

She purrs
with
satisfaction...

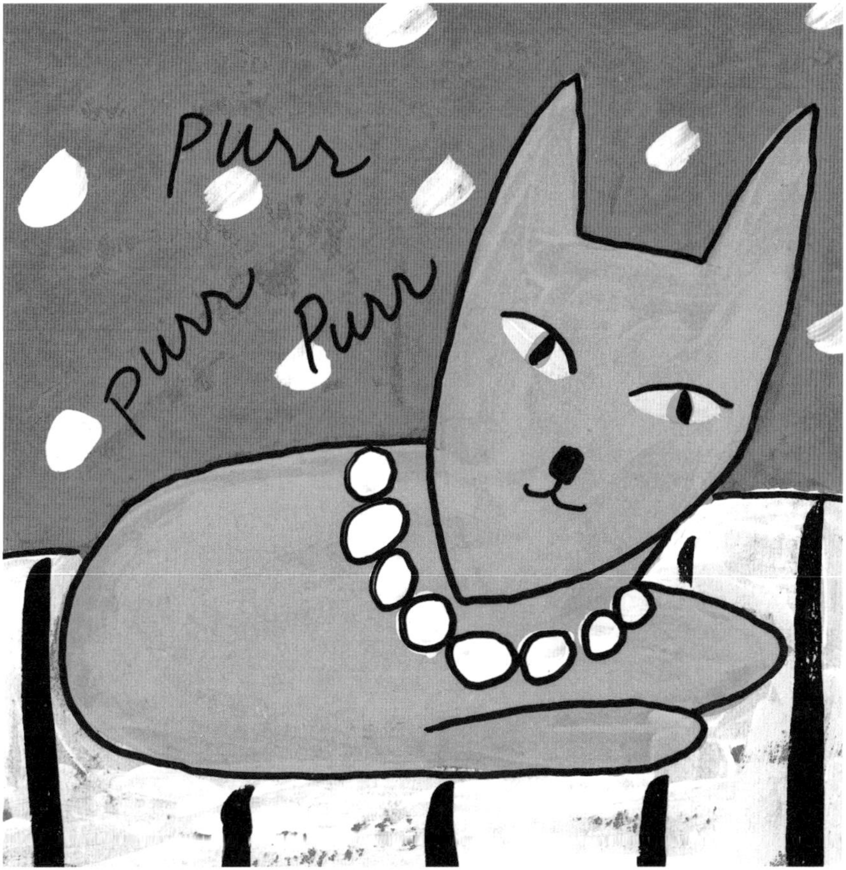
Purr
Purr
Purr

she is the
fairest,
by far.

She pampers herself and when she's seen

her coat
is brilliant
with a
perfect sheen.

Each day she leisurely naps on top of the chair.

She leaves
behind her
fur...
and doesn't
seem to care.

She suns
herself
in the
afternoon.

Oblivious
to the flowers
that need
light to bloom.

My cat
must be of
royal
descent.

I think it's
true —
my cat forgets
who pays the
rent.

She eats only
caviar
when she's
ready to dine.

I love my cat... but, I wonder, is her life better than mine?

Pictures and verse by Sandra Magsamen
© 2001 Hanny Girl Productions, Inc.

Published in 2001 by
Stewart, Tabori & Chang
A division of Harry N. Abrams, Inc.
115 West 18th Street
New York, NY 10011

Distributed in Canada by
General Publishing Company Ltd.
30 Lesmill Road
Don Mills, Ontario, Canada M3B 2J6

ISBN: 1-58479-066-0

Printed in Hong Kong

10 9 8 7 6 5 4 3 2 1